Richard Trevithick

An illustrated life of Richard Trevithick

1771-1833

James Hodge

Shire Publications Ltd

Contents

Early history of the steam engine 5
Boyhood and first working days 11
The high-pressure engine and the locomotive 17
New projects and inventions 24
South American adventure 34
Return home 40
Chronology 46
Bibliography 47
Index 48

ACKNOWLEDGEMENTS

The author and publishers wish to thank the following for permitting the reproduction of the illustrations on the pages indicated: Radio Times Hulton Picture Library: 38; Trustees of the Science Museum, London: front cover, 2, 7, 16, 25, 31; also the following which are Crown Copyright: 23 (lower), 27, 33; K. A. Tanner: 4, 8, 9, 19 (lower), 45; G.A.C. Dart, City of Cardiff Public Libraries: 13 (upper); R. E. Trevithick: 10. Illustrations on the following pages were reproduced from Francis Trevithick's 'Life of Richard Trevithick', 1872: 13 (lower), 19 (upper), 31 (lower), 39, 43.

Published in 1995 by Shire Publications Ltd, Cromwell House, Church Street, Princes Risborough, Buckinghamshire HP27 9AA, UK.
Copyright © 1973 by James Hodge. First published 1973. Reprinted 1978, 1984, 1989 and 1995. ISBN 0 85263 177 4.

Printed in Great Britain by CIT Printing Services, Press Buildings, Merlins Bridge, Haverfordwest, Dyfed SA61 1XF.

Front cover and opposite: A portrait in oil of Richard Trevithick by J. Linnell, 1816. (Trustees of the Science Museum, London.)

Richard Trevithick

This bronze statue of Trevithick stands in front of the public library at Camborne. The sculptor was L.E.Merrifield.

Early history of the steam engine

THE CORNISH MINES

Tin and copper have been used by man since remote times, particularly in the manufacture of bronze, an alloy of these two metals which is much harder than either of them used separately. The extraction of the ores from the earth has long been a way of life in Cornwall. At first they were obtained by alluvial working, but when the surface deposits were exhausted man began to dig ever deeper for his metal, and the deeper he dug the greater were the problems that he encountered and the higher the cost of the ore. By the latter part of the seventeenth century the Cornish miners were digging deep and towards the end of the nineteenth century, when alluvial deposits were discovered and worked much more cheaply elsewhere in the world, the industry in Cornwall fell into decline. Many pits closed and the miners were forced to emigrate all over the world, anywhere that work could be found. The visitor to Cornwall today will find two mines that have continued in production, South Crofty near Camborne and Geevor at Pendeen, and he will see, too, the signs of a revival in the industry with the recently opened shafts at Wheal Jane and elsewhere.

At the time when Richard Trevithick was born in 1771, near Carn Brea in the parish of Illogan, between Camborne and Redruth, in the heart of the mining country, many men, and women too, were employed in the extraction of the ores. But as the miners were forced to follow the lodes downwards into the ground, apart from the obvious difficulties and dangers of digging deep, the pumping out of the water that accumulated in the workings was one of the major problems they encountered. The difficulty lay not so much in designing and building the actual pumps needed, but in providing the power to drive them. Until early in the eighteenth century animal power, windmills and water-wheels had been the only sources of power, apart from the efforts of the workers themselves. The solution of this problem had occupied many men before him, and to understand the nature and importance of the contribution that Trevithick made to engineering, it is necessary to look briefly at the work of some of them.

Thomas Savery, a Devon man, had devised a simple form of pump, operated directly by the pressure of steam on the water being raised. This, though very crude and inefficient, achieved a certain amount of success for a while, and was known as the 'Miner's Friend'. It was not, however, an idea which could be developed into a more efficient and powerful pump, nor could it be used for any purpose other than pumping water.

THOMAS NEWCOMEN AND JAMES WATT

The real forerunner of the whole family of steam engines which was developed over the next two hundred years was the one built by another Devonian, Thomas Newcomen of Dartmouth. The first one known to have been used for pumping was installed in a coal mine at Dudley Castle in Staffordshire in 1712. Newcomen was an ironmonger: in those days this meant that he made, as well as sold, iron merchandise such as tools. He regularly visited the Cornish mines and very soon his engine was adopted in these too. Apart from the comparative crudity of its construction, which was not surprising when one remembers that it was the first real engine ever made and must have posed formidable manufacturing as well as design problems, the interesting thing about it is its close similarity to the beam engines that were built up until the beginning of the present century. It had all the fundamental features. A boiler supplied steam to a cylinder in which a piston slid up and down: the piston was attached to one end of a large beam (a wooden one in this case) which was pivoted at its centre, and the pump was connected to the other end of the beam. The valve gear which controlled the admission of steam to the cylinder and which was operated by the engine itself, was a particularly important feature: it meant that once the engine had been started, and so long as it was kept supplied with fuel and water, it would operate of its own accord. This is one of the essential features of what we call an engine.

The importance of the introduction of Newcomen's engine was not so much for its immediate effect on mining, great

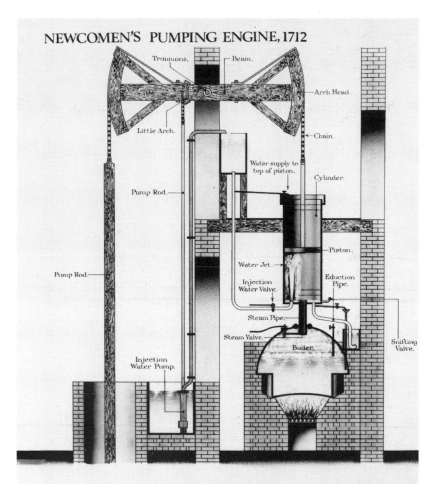

NEWCOMEN'S PUMPING ENGINE, 1712

This diagram shows a typical atmospheric pumping engine, as made by Newcomen, in section, with the piston in the middle of the downward or working stroke. Steam is generated at atmospheric pressure in the boiler and fills the cylinder during the upward stroke of the piston. The steam valve is then closed and the steam is condensed by a jet of cold water causing a vacuum under the piston. The atmospheric pressure acting on the top of the piston forces it down, hence the name "atmospheric" engine, and this constitutes the working stroke. The piston is raised again by the overbalancing weight of the pump-rods.

though this was, but because it showed the possibility of generating mechanical power from heat. This is, of course, what we still do today, not only in steam turbines but in petrol and diesel engines, jet engines and even in nuclear power plants.

Just two years before Trevithick's birth came the next significant step in the development of the steam engine. In 1769 James Watt invented the separate condenser. Newcomen's engine had actually derived its power from the action of atmospheric pressure on the top of the piston, and was therefore known as an 'atmospheric' engine. The steam which filled the cylinder below the piston was condensed by injecting cold water into it, so creating a vacuum and allowing the atmospheric pressure above the piston to force it downwards. This process was very wasteful of heat because the whole cylinder had to be heated and cooled on every stroke. James Watt realised this and condensed the steam in a separate vessel, so that there was no cooling of the cylinder itself. This greatly increased the efficiency of the engine, and Watt and his business

The cottage in which Richard Trevithick once lived at Penponds near Camborne.

The 90" cylinder pumping engine at Taylor's shaft, East Pool and Agar Mine, Pool, Redruth. It was built by Harvey's of Hayle in 1892 and has been restored by the Cornish Engines Preservation Society. The engine is now in the care of the National Trust.

partner Matthew Boulton also brought in many mechanical and manufacturing improvements which resulted in much more widespread use of steam engines—not only for pumping water out of the mines but for driving all kinds of machinery in factories and elsewhere. Watt's engines were more powerful and could operate at higher speeds, more reliably, and using only about a third as much coal as Newcomen's.

As Trevithick grew up, the engines built by James Watt were the basis of his experience and thinking and it is not possible to appreciate the magnitude of the changes that he was to make without knowing what he found when he began to work.

A miniature of Richard Trevithick as a young man.

Boyhood and first working days

SCHOOLDAYS AND EARLY LIFE IN CORNWALL

Richard Trevithick senior was a mine 'captain', a position similar to a manager's today, but it included responsibility for the pumping engines. In his work he had to deal with a number of both Newcomen and Watt engines, and so he probably knew as much about them from an operational viewpoint as anyone. He had married in 1760 Anne Teague, a member of a Redruth family, many of whom were mine managers. Their son Richard, born on 13th April 1771, was the youngest but one of their six children, and the only boy. It is thought that Anne Trevithick indulged and spoilt her only son. Young Richard was sent to the village school in Camborne, and though the kind of education provided there was no doubt very elementary, he evidently did not take much advantage of it and the master reported him as 'a disobedient, slow, obstinate, spoiled boy, frequently absent and very inattentive'. He did show an aptitude for arithmetic, but arrived at the right answers by unconventional and, no doubt, unpopular means. Soon he left school and spent most of his time wandering around the mines, accepted the more easily by the miners, we may think, because of the widespread respect in which his father was held. He had no formal theoretical education, but what he saw and heard in the mines probably provided the best training a boy of his talents and energies could have had. He learned a great deal about the practical problems of mining, and about the erection, operation and maintenance of engines and pumps.

James Watt not only sold his engines to the Cornish mines, he charged a royalty, as he was quite entitled to do. This levy was based on the saving of coal used in one of his engines compared with a Newcomen engine of the same power, and the charge was equivalent to a third of the saving. So although the mine owners enjoyed two thirds of the saving, together with the use of more reliable and powerful machines, after a while they began to feel aggrieved by having to pay the other third. This was especially so

11

when the life of Watt's patent was extended until 1800, a total of thirty-one years.

Towards the end of this period great efforts were made by a number of Cornish engineers to design engines which, though equally efficient, would avoid the separate condenser patent. None of these attempts was successful, but they did result in a number of new ideas being tried out, and they set Richard Trevithick thinking of different ways of using steam to drive engines. Without the stimulus of the Cornish attitude to Watt and his engines, he might not have achieved so much so quickly.

By the time he was fifteen years old, there were twenty-one Watt engines working in the county, the first being installed in 1780. As there were still a few Newcomen-type 'atmospheric' engines working until 1790 he must have seen as wide a variety of engines in operation as was possible at that time.

Richard grew up a very big and strong young man. He was six feet two inches tall and broad in proportion, and as the Cornish were generally rather short and stocky in build, his size must have been much more noticeable than it would be today. His strength was enormous and was for long a legend. There are many stories of his physical prowess. It is said that he would stand on top of the head gear of a mine, swinging a sledge-hammer about his head for exercise, and that he could throw a sledge-hammer from the ground clean over the top of an engine-house. He could write his name on a beam six feet from the floor, with half a hundredweight hanging from his thumb, and it is told that on one occasion when several young men were trying to lift a large pump barrel of seven or eight hundredweight, Richard came along, picked it up and walked off with it on his shoulder. The picture emerges of a strong and exuberant young man; there was an occasion after one of the monthly dinners at Dolcoath mine, at which the shareholders were paid their dividends, when he picked up another mine engineer, Hodge by name, himself a well-built man, and seizing him round the waist put his boots against the ceiling.

Like many big men he was gentle and kindly in his dealings with other people. Many years later an old lady with whose parents Trevithick had lodged while he was working on an engine at Ding Dong mine told his son Francis: 'He was a great favourite, full of fun and good humour, and a good story teller.' But he was sometimes quick to take offence if the value or quality of his work was questioned.

Above: Trevithick's birthplace near Carn Brea, Cornwall, as it appeared in 1871.

Below: The high-pressure expansive steam condensing Whim-engine that Trevithick erected at Cook's Kitchen in 1800.

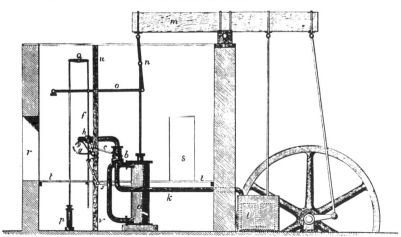

EARLY INVENTIONS

Trevithick's first employment was at the age of nineteen, at East Stray Park mine near Camborne. In 1792 he was asked to report on the performance of a new engine built at Tincroft mine. He had evidently already acquired a reputation, to be employed as a consulting engineer at so early an age; the report that he made is still in existence. He very soon became involved in attempts being made to avoid the Watt separate condenser patent, and Watt at one time obtained an injunction to stop him from erecting or operating one of these locally designed engines, regarding the young Trevithick as his chief enemy in Cornwall.

It was while Trevithick was in London, engaged in a patent action in 1796, that he first met Davies Giddy (later Gilbert), another Cornishman, who became his friend and adviser, and remained so for the rest of his life. Gilbert was not an engineer, but he was a man of very considerable scientific and mathematical ability—he later became President of the Royal Society, following Humphry Davy (yet another Cornishman) in that office. Davies Gilbert helped and advised a number of engineers and scientists, among them Telford and Davy, but most of all Trevithick, who kept up a correspondence with him over many years and often asked him for his opinion on the feasibility of new ideas.

Trevithick senior died in 1797, and later that year the young Richard married Jane Harvey of Hayle. She was a member of the family that built up the foundry there and that made the biggest and some of the most efficient beam engines ever built anywhere. Jane was a woman of great courage and strong character, attributes that served her in good stead in the years to come, when her husband was often away from home, leaving her to manage the family affairs alone, and when his financial position was often precarious. She stood by him all her life.

It was at about the time of his marriage that Trevithick's inventive mind began to be most active; from then until he left for South America in 1816 was a period of brilliant original thought, ceaseless activity and apparently inexhaustible energy.

He worked on the plunger pole pump, a simple and very practical form of pump to be used in conjunction with a beam engine. Although the basic idea was not new, his design was a considerable improvement on anything that had gone before and soon it was in widespread use. He also reversed the plunger pole pump, turning it into a water-power engine—again it was the practical points of design that made this a much better machine than its predecessors. Another improvement, of local benefit, was the egg-shaped iron 'kibbal' or bucket for raising ore in a shaft. Because of its shape and construction this was a much more practical proposition than the iron-bound wooden tubs previously in use.

Trevithick's friend and adviser Davies Gilbert. An engraving of the portrait by Henry Howard, R.A.

Trevithick's experimental model road locomotive, 1797-8.

The high-pressure engine and the locomotive

HIGH-PRESSURE ENGINES

However, it was his work on the steam engine that was of major importance. In 1797 Trevithick made his first models of high-pressure engines, first a stationary one and then a little locomotive (which is believed to be the one now in the Science Museum). In these, steam exhausting from the cylinder went straight to atmosphere—there was no condenser and they avoided the Watt patent. But they did much more than this—the use of high-pressure steam enabled them to produce much more power for the same size of cylinder. In addition, they could run much faster, again increasing their output. Weight and size were also reduced by the absence of the condenser and its accessories, and the whole layout of the engine was simplified by doing away with the beam and driving a shaft directly through a crank. Davies Gilbert recounts: 'On one occasion Trevithick came to me and inquired with great eagerness as to what I apprehended would be loss of power in working an engine by the force of steam, raised to the pressure of several atmospheres but instead of condensing to let the steam escape. I of course answered at once that the loss of power would be one atmosphere, diminished power by the saving of an airpump with its friction, and in many cases with the raising of condensing water. I never saw a man more delighted, and I believe that within a month several puffers were in actual work.' Certainly Trevithick was not one to let the grass grow under his foot when he had a new idea, and the 'puffers' were probably first used for winding ore at Dolcoath. They were so called because of the noise made by the escaping exhaust steam—as in a steam locomotive.

Watt had thought of using high-pressure steam but had not pursued the idea because of mechanical difficulties and danger, as well as the loss of power if no condenser was used. Murdoch, Watt's resident engineer in Cornwall, had made a model steam locomotive in Redruth in 1786; it is possible, though the evidence is confused, that Trevithick had seen or knew of this model. But he almost certainly did not know of the two locomotives built in France by Cugnot in 1769 and 1770. These were undoubtedly the first self-propelled vehicles in the world, but they did not perform very well and no further developments were based on them.

TREVITHICK'S ROAD LOCOMOTIVE

The first full-sized locomotive in Britain was the one built by Trevithick at Camborne in 1801. An essential preliminary was an experiment that he carried out with Davies Gilbert to determine whether, if the wheels were driven via the axle, the friction between their rims and the road would be sufficient to prevent slipping. They borrowed the only one-horse chaise available for hire west of Truro (the same one, incidentally, that had been used by Watt when he had visited the county sixteen years before), and propelled it up various hills on the outskirts of Camborne by the turning of the wheels. Satisfied on this point, Trevithick went ahead with the building of his steam road carriage. Its exact form is not known, but it probably had a wooden chassis, a boiler with a fairly tall chimney, and a single-cylinder engine mounted in the boiler and driving one pair of wheels through a crank.

The first run was made on Christmas Eve 1801 and the locomotive successfully carried a number of men up a hill. The life of this historic machine was very short: on 28th December it was being driven along a country road just outside Camborne, with Trevithick's cousin, Andrew Vivian, steering—Vivian collaborated with him in this and in several other ventures—when, passing over a gully in the road, the steering handle was jerked from Captain Andrew's hand, the locomotive went out of control and broke down. As related by Gilbert: 'The carriage was forced under some shelter, and the Parties adjourned to the Hotel, & comforted their Hearts with a Roast Goose and proper drinks, when, forgetfull of the Engine, its Water boiled away, the Iron became red hot, and nothing that was combustible remained either of the Engine or the house.'

Undismayed by the loss of this locomotive, Trevithick went to London, to take out, with Vivian, a patent incorporating not only the features of this machine, but additional ones as well. After building another small stationary engine, operating at the

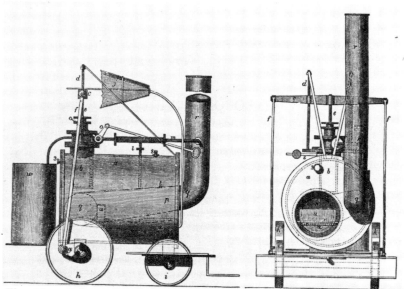

The side and front elevations of Trevithick's Camborne road locomotive. From a drawing by Francis Trevithick.

The plaque at Camborne commemorating the site where the locomotive was built and began its run in 1801.

A drawing of Trevithick's high-pressure engine and boiler. From John Farey's 'Treatise on the Steam Engine', Vol II c 1840.

then unheard-of pressure of 145 lb per sq.in. at Coalbrookdale in Shropshire, he and Vivian put in hand another road carriage. The engine was made at Hayle and the carriage in London, where it ran in 1803. From a variety of sources it is known that it made a number of quite long journeys about the capital, but strangely it was not mentioned in the press of the time. Seeing no return for their efforts, Cap'n Dick and Cap'n Andrew gave up.

Trevithick was kept very busy arranging the supply of high-pressure stationary engines for a wide variety of uses, and had he been capable of organising his affairs on a proper business footing, there is no doubt that he could have become financially successful at this time. His high-pressure engines were well designed and reliable, and there was a great need for them. Many of them lasted a very long time; one of the earliest, installed at Cook's Kitchen near Camborne in 1800, was still working in 1870. In 1803 he suffered a serious setback: one of his engines was in use in Greenwich, pumping the water out of the foundations of a corn mill being built there, when the boiler burst, killing four men. The accident was entirely due to carelessness in operation, but much was made of it, to Trevithick's disadvantage. He wrote of it in a letter to Davies Gilbert, from Penydaren on 1st October 1803: 'It appears the boy that had the care of the engine was gon to catch eales in the foundation of the building, and left the care of it to one of the Labourers; this labourer saw the engine working much faster than usual, stop'd it without takeing off a spanner which fastned down the steam lever, and a short time after being Idle it burst. It killed 3 on the spot and one other is sence dead of his wounds. The boy returned at the instant and was going to take off the trigg from the valve. He was hurt, but is now on recovery; he had left the engine about an hour ... I beleive that Mr B. [Boulton] & Watt is abt to do mee every engurey in their power for the[y] have don their outemost to repoart the exploseion both in the newspapers and private letters very different to what it really is ...'

Trevithick reacted to Boulton and Watt's attempt to evidence the dangers of high-pressure steam, by fitting a variety of safety devices, which effectively prevented further accidents. These were a lead fusible plug, a mercury-filled pressure gauge so proportioned that if the pressure became excessive it blew out the mercury, allowing the steam to escape and making plenty of noise in the process, and duplicate safety valves.

TREVITHICK'S RAILWAY LOCOMOTIVES

A share of the patent for these machines was sold in 1803 to Samuel Homfray, an ironmaster of Penydaren in South Wales. Homfray was a keen supporter of the high-pressure engine and as well as helping to increase sales, he made a bet with Anthony Hill, a neighbouring ironmaster, of 500 guineas even money that a steam locomotive could haul 10 tons of iron on the tramway (usually horse-drawn) from Penydaren to Abercynon, a distance of 9¾ miles. On 13th February 1804 the locomotive ran for the first time, and on 21st February Trevithick handsomely won the bet for Mr Homfray. Davies Gilbert was told of this success: 'Yesterday we proceeded on our journey with the engine; we carry'd ten tons of Iron, five waggons, and 70 Men riding on them the whole of the journey. Its above nine miles which we perform'd in 4 hours & 5 Mints, but we had to cut down som trees and remove some large rocks out of road. The engine, while working, went nearly 5 miles pr hour; there was no water put into the boiler from the time we started untill we arriv'd.'

This was a most historic occasion in the development of the railway. Trevithick's locomotive was certainly the first to run on rails. It had coupled wheels which were smooth and relied on friction to transmit the drive. The high-pressure steam was non-condensing, and the exhaust steam was used to help the draught through the fire-box. In fact it had most of the essential features of the engines which lasted for the whole steam era. Though the Penydaren engine was not used for long on the tramway, mainly because its weight was too much for the cast-iron rails, it was undoubtedly the forerunner of the much better-known engines which were built by the Stephensons at the beginning of the commercial development of the railways—*Blucher, Locomotion* and *Rocket.*

Another engine very similar to the Penydaren one was built in 1805 at Newcastle-on-Tyne, not by Trevithick but to his design and instructions. This did not run on rails as intended, for the wooden wagon ways were even less suitable for its weight than the cast-iron ones in Wales, and the coal-owners still found it cheaper to buy horse fodder. There is little doubt though that George Stephenson saw this machine and that he and Trevithick met at some time. Trevithick's last attempt to exploit the locomotive was made in London in 1808 when a new engine known as *Catch me who can* was built and ran on a circular track near Gower Street. It was apparently intended to show that it could travel further, faster than a horse. Admission to the enclosure was one shilling, which included a ride for those who dared. This venture too failed because of the inadequate strength of the track.

Trevithick's real reason for being in Penydaren in the first place was not to build the locomotive, but to supply engines for the ironworks and colliery. This he did to good effect, some of his engines installed there being still at work fifty years later. He now plunged into other projects, mainly applications of the high-pressure engine. These covered an astonishingly wide range, including boring brass cannon, crushing stone, powering rolling mills, corn and grist mills, forge hammers, stamps and blast-furnace blowers as well as the original mining uses. He drove a barge by paddle-wheels driven by a steam engine, and several dredgers. These were not the first of their kind, but were probably the first to use the compact high-pressure engines.

*Below: a drawing by Rowlandson
of the 'Catch me who can'
locomotive running on a circular
railway laid down by Trevithick in
1808 on a site which is now
Torrington Square, near Euston
Station. Right: an admission ticket
to the railway. Admission to the
enclosure was one shilling,
including a ride for those who
dared.*

23

New projects and inventions

THE THAMES DRIFTWAY

In 1805 a plan was made by a number of gentlemen, 'One Body Politick and Corporate, by the Name and Style of the Thames Archway Company', to drive a tunnel under the Thames, 'capable of taking horses and cattle, with or without carriages, and foot passengers'. Until this time there had been no tunnels under a major waterway. A Cornish engineer, Robert Vazie, was selected to carry out the work on the Thames Archway, which was to go from Rotherhithe to a point on the north bank of the river, near the entrance to the Regents Canal Dock. Vazie planned to sink a shaft close to the south bank of the river and, when he had got down to the right level, to drive a small tunnel or driftway to explore the ground and to serve as a drain for the eventual tunnel. Vazie encountered great difficulties in sinking his shaft to about 70 feet deep, due to the influx of water and quicksand, and progress was exceedingly slow. The directors of the company did not agree with Vazie as to the further conduct of the work, and eventually Trevithick was introduced to them by Vazie. (It is thought likely that Davjes Gilbert had suggested Trevithick, when Vazie appealed to him for advice.)

The proprietors agreed to pay Trevithick £1,000 if he could carry the driftway to the north shore, or £500 if they ordered work to stop in the middle, but nothing if he did not succeed in completing it. He began to drive from the bottom of the shaft in August 1807, working in a very small section only 5 feet high, 3 feet wide at the bottom and 2 feet 6 inches at the top, inside the timber lining. It must have been extremely difficult for the men to work there, and to pass each other. The total distance which Trevithick estimated that it would have to be extended from the bottom of the southern shaft to the corresponding one to be sunk on the north shore was 1,220 feet. On 23rd December when the drift had progressed some 950 feet, there was a sudden inrush of water from a quicksand.

This was dealt with but only a month later, at a distance of 1,040 feet from the south bank, the river broke in due to a fall of earth into the drift. Trevithick was very nearly drowned by the break-in, being the last to leave, but he made further great efforts to push the driftway onwards by having clay thrown in over the hole in the river bed. After draining the drift, flat iron bars were driven ahead of the working face and the water was tapped from the quicksand by means of iron pipes. This effected a further advance of 12 feet, but by this time the directors had lost their nerve. Some of them were very much prejudiced against Trevithick, and did all they could to discredit him. To pacify them the majority of the directors, who still had confidence in his abilities and integrity, called in two experienced colliery engineers from the North of England to look into the situation and make a report. In this, they fully supported Trevithick, and one of their answers was: 'He has shown most extraordinary skill and ingenuity in passing the quicksand, and we do not know any practical miner that we think more competent to the task than he is. We judge from the

A conjectural model now in the Science Museum, London, of Trevithick's Penydaren locomotive of 1804.

work itself, and until this occasion of viewing the work, we did not know Mr Trevithick.'

Trevithick prepared to overcome the new difficulties by means of a coffer-dam placed over the driftway, in the river, but though this would probably have succeeded he was not allowed to carry it out. The work came to a standstill and there was much wrangling—he eventually proposed that a fresh approach should be made, by building the final tunnel (using the driftway as a drain as originally intended) in sections in a trench dug in the bottom of the river from a caisson. This would be advanced as the tunnel was completed. His first suggestion was for a brick lining to the tunnel, but later this was changed to cast-iron sections. Although the idea was approved by Trevithick's well-known friend Simon Goodrich, of the Inspector General's Department of the Navy Board, the directors did not pursue it and Trevithick's connection with the Thames tunnel virtually ceased. He had failed, but only just, and in the face of enormous difficulties, many of which he had managed to overcome.

To Sir Marc Isambard Brunel and his son, Isambard Kingdom Brunel, came the triumph of completing the first tunnel under the Thames: three quarters of a mile upstream from the Thames Archway, it was started by Brunel senior in 1823 and finished by his son in 1843. In its construction it too suffered a number of catastrophic floodings, nearly drowning Isambard Kingdom on at least one occasion.

The submerged tube that Trevithick suggested was not used for many years, the first time being across the Detroit river in Michigan in 1906-9, and most recently under the harbour in Hong Kong. This type of construction has also received serious consideration as one possible method for the Channel tunnel.

As Richard Trevithick seemed likely to be in London for a long time, he finally persuaded his wife Jane with their four children (there were eventually six) to join him; this she did in 1808. She had been by no means enthusiastic but she did come, only to find on her arrival two of her letters to her husband, unopened in his pocket. His reply, on being taxed with this, was simply: 'You know, Jane, that your notes were full of reasons for not coming to London, and I had not the heart to read any more of them.' Their stay in the capital, which lasted for two and a half years, was not a happy one; their lodgings, first in Rotherhithe and then in Limehouse, were not to be compared with their home in Cornwall, and their affairs did not prosper for long at a time.

PARTNERSHIP WITH DICKINSON

Following his failure with the driftway, the engineer turned his attention to the locomotive *Catch-me-who-can,* already mentioned. In 1808 he entered into some sort of partnership with one Robert Dickinson. Little is known about Dickinson except that he is described as a West India merchant and that he was concerned with a large number and variety of patents. It appears likely that he provided the capital to take out patents on some of Trevithick's ideas, and to exploit them. Perhaps the word 'exploit' may be particularly appropriate, as Dickinson eventually left his partner to bear the brunt of bankruptcy proceedings, when in all likelihood Trevithick had been relying on him for the financial conduct of their affairs. Richard had made a number of interesting inventions, some of which proved to be very useful and successful, either then or later. First of these was the 'Nautical Labourer', a steam tug and floating crane propelled by paddle-wheel. It was never brought to commercial use, partly because of the fire regulations obtaining in the docks, and partly because the Society of Coal Whippers

This high-pressure engine made by Hazledine & Co. of Bridgnorth c 1805 is a typical example of the engines Trevithick was designing at about this time.

27

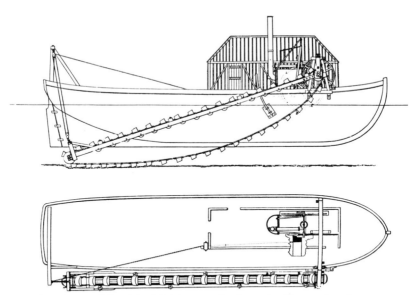

*Two plan views of Trevithick's Thames dredger. An illustration from
Rees's 'Cyclopedia' of 1819. The engine powered a chain of buckets that
emptied ballast into waiting barges.*

protested against the encouragement of such a rival, declined to
work with it, and threatened to drown its inventor. Trevithick
was guarded by policemen, two of them keeping watch at his
house. He had ideas, too, for a land-based mobile crane which
would also be able to double as a fire pump.

Later that same year another of his patents covered the use
of iron tanks for stowing cargo and water in ships, instead of
the hitherto universal wooden casks. This was a real advance
and it was not difficult to develop and achieve acceptance of it.
A story is told of the origin of this idea by his eldest son
Richard who was ten years old at the time: 'When a little boy,
shortly after reaching London from Cornwall, about 1808, my
Father on coming into the house on a Sunday morning, desired
me to fetch a wine-glass, and taking me by the hand, walked to
the old yard near the tunnel works. There was an old
steam-engine boiler in the yard: my Father filled the glass with
water from the boiler gauge-cock, and asked me to tell him if it
was good water. We used to speak of this as the origin of the
iron tanks.'

A small works was established at Limehouse, where the family was then living, to make these tanks: three men were employed but it seems that the business was not profitable because there were disagreements between Trevithick and Dickinson and they both left too much to the men. The tanks were also used as 'camels' for raising sunken ships, by attaching them under the water to the vessel to be raised and then pumping air into them to displace the water, thus giving sufficient buoyancy to bring the whole to the surface. In 1810 a wreck was raised off Margate by this means, with the inventor in charge of operations. When the ship had been successfully raised and was being taken into shallow waters, a dispute arose with the owners over payment: Trevithick, impetuous as always, cast loose the lashings and let the ship sink to the bottom again. Once more, he had failed to make any money. Later Maudslay took up the manufacture of the iron tanks.

Another patent, in 1809, covered a vast range of ideas for improvements to ships and their equipment, including iron floating docks, iron ships, tubular telescopic iron masts, yards and bowsprits, a method of seasoning and bending timber in hot flue gases, a wooden hull structure with diagonal ribs, iron buoys, ovens in a boiler to permit cooking at sea and others. Models of some of them were made, and some iron buoys, but little else.

In May 1810 Richard Trevithick had an attack of typhus and very nearly died; not until September was he well enough to be moved and then he was taken back to Cornwall by sea; this journey was an adventure in itself as the ship was chased by a French warship, but fortunately escaped. His illness was followed by another serious setback, when he and Dickinson were declared bankrupt in February 1811. After a great deal of trouble, added to by the unscrupulous actions of Dickinson, he received his discharge in 1814, having apparently paid off most of the debts of the partnership by himself.

THE CORNISH BOILER AND THE CORNISH ENGINE

In the meantime his powers of invention reasserted themselves and he made a number of contributions to the development of the steam engine. Among other innovations of this period, the first and best-known was the Cornish boiler. The earliest examples were installed as replacements to drive

Boulton and Watt pumping engines at Dolcoath (about 1812). They were horizontal, cylindrical boilers with the fire tube passing through the middle, also horizontally. They represented a very great improvement on previous types, both mechanically and thermally, and were very widely used. They were later joined by the Lancashire boiler, which was similar in construction, but had twin fire tubes. The low-pressure engines needed modification to enable them to use the boiler's output effectively, but eventually the efficiency of the Dolcoath plant was more than doubled.

Next, in 1812, came the first application of high-pressure steam used expansively and condensing, generated by his Cornish boiler—this was to an experimental engine at Wheal Prosper and it is considered to have been the first 'Cornish engine', the type that was to become so well-known all over the world. For a long period it was the most efficient kind of steam engine in existence. Many other engineers in Cornwall contributed to its development over the years, but there is no doubt that it was Trevithick's work that was decisive.

In the same year he built the first of his very simple but highly effective high-pressure rotative engines, non-condensing, for Sir Christopher Hawkins of Probus. It was used on the farm to drive a corn threshing machine and in this it was most successful and much cheaper to run than the horses it replaced. For nearly seventy years it continued to work and it is now preserved in the Science Museum. Other similar machines were built for use in the West Country and elsewhere. Although there is no record of any being built, at about the same time Trevithick made a drawing of a machine somewhat similar to a modern rotary cultivator. It had a four-wheeled chassis, to be pulled to and fro across a field by a stationary steam engine (a technique long used for steam ploughing), and the rotation of the back axle drove, through gearing, a shovel wheel. This chopped up and threw sideways the soil which had been sliced up by straight cutters.

Various schemes had been put forward to protect the anchorage at Plymouth from southerly gales and eventually, at the request of the Admiralty, Sir John Rennie prepared a report on the various proposals. This was in 1806, but it was not until five years later that work on a breakwater was put in hand. Large quantities of stone were needed for its construction, and 25 acres of land were bought three miles away, from which it

In the Science Museum, London, is the above high-pressure engine and boiler used for thrashing corn. It was built by Trevithick in 1812 for Sir Christopher Hawkins of Trewithen. Left is a drawing, by his son Francis Trevithick, of Trevithick's steam cultivator.

was to be quarried. With his friend Rastrick, Trevithick went to see the works in November 1812. They were not impressed with what they saw, and very soon Trevithick had produced a number of ideas for improvements, notably an engine-driven machine for boring holes in the limestone. He claimed that this could drill holes five times as fast as could be done by hand; it is to be regretted that we have no details of this, although we know that later he referred to a twist bit of some kind which cleared the chippings from the hole. He also suggested the use of plug and feathers for splitting the rock from the solid mass in the form of square-cornered blocks. By the use of 'feathers', which are wedge-shaped pieces of iron, the splitting force can be applied by the main wedge at the bottom of the hole if necessary, and spread over a bigger area, so that local breakdown of the stone does not happen before it splits as desired. There were also suggestions for the use of steam engines to lift and move the blocks of stone, and it is likely that some of these ideas were in fact put into practice, as the price allowed in the contract for winning the stone was greatly decreased soon afterwards.

Of a flood of new ideas and actual machines built about this time, mention should be made of his plunger pole high-pressure engines, which were successful; the last of them, installed at Herland mine in 1812, was the one of which he was proudest; it approached three times the efficiency of the best Watt engines.

The sheer volume of work that Trevithick undertook, the drawings that were made, the letters written and the travelling done in the supervision of the building of his machines impress us with his determination, impatience of difficulties and an almost superhuman mental and physical energy. An account of difficulties met with in the starting up of the engine at Herland was recorded in a lively manner by one Henry Phillips in his reminiscences in 1869:

' I was a boy working in the mine, and several of us peeped in at the door to see what was doing. Captain Dick was in a great way, the engine would not start; after a bit Captain Dick threw himself down upon the floor of the engine-house, and there he lay upon his back; then up he jumped, and snatched a sledge-hammer out of the hands of a man who was driving in a wedge, and lashed it home in a minute. There never was a man could use a sledge like Captain Dick; he was as strong as a bull. Then, he picked up a spanner and unscrewed something, and off she went. Captain Vivian was near me, looking in at the doorway; Captain Dick saw him and, shaking his fist, said "If you come in here I'll throw you down the shaft". I suppose Captain Vivian had something to do with making the boilers, and Captain Dick was angry because they leaked clouds of steam. You could hardly see, or hear anybody speak in the engine-house, it was so full of steam and noise.'

Trevithick then built what he called a recoil engine. It was very similar to the aeolipile of Hero of Alexandria (about 120 B.C.)– though very much bigger. It was rather like an enormous catherine wheel; two hollow arms emitted steam at high velocity from their tips, at opposite ends of a diameter. They were pivoted in the middle and steam was supplied through a hollow axle. The first version was 15 feet in diameter and a later one 24 feet they must have been a fearsome sight. It was his intention to use this crude form of reaction turbine to drive a ship, through a propeller, but apart from running the engine, we do not know how the project progressed. He soon realised from correspondence with Davies Gilbert that the speed would have to be much higher than was practicable in order to obtain anything like a reasonable efficiency. His propeller, not the first of its kind, was not likely to perform well as it was more screw than propeller.

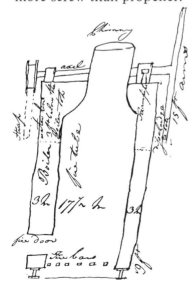

Trevithick's sketch of his recoil engine and boiler, 1815. It was referred to as 'the windmill' by his workmen who thought it a device for throwing missiles.

South American adventure

THE PERUVIAN SILVER MINES

Trevithick, now in his early forties, had been working as an engineer to the mines in Cornwall since his return to his native county from London, following his attack of typhus, but events taking place far from England were to have a profound effect on the rest of his life. They began in Peru.

The ancient and very rich silver mines at Cerro de Pasco had fallen into a state of decay, largely for lack of adequate means of removing the water from the workings. A man of Swiss origin, Francisco Uvillé, had discussed with some local merchants the possibility of using steam engines to pump out the water, and in 1811 he was sent to England to find out if this could be done. On arrival he got in touch with the firm of Boulton and Watt and they, quite rightly, told him that their engines would not be suitable. Not only would the low-pressure type not work effectively at the required altitude, the mines being 14,000 feet above sea level, but it would not be possible to make it in small enough or light enough pieces to be transported on the mule track (which in places rose to a height of 17,000 feet). It was quite by chance that Uvillé saw in a shop window in London a model of a Trevithick high-pressure steam engine. This he bought for the sum of twenty guineas, and he took it back with him to Peru. It was found to work satisfactorily at Cerro de Pasco and Uvillé and two of his associates formed a company to drain the Pasco mines. He then set sail again for England, but was taken ill on board and landed at Jamaica. Being sufficiently recovered to continue his journey, he took passage in the Falmouth packet *Fox*. On board he talked to fellow passengers of his mission, and his intention to try to find Richard Trevithick in England. As luck would have it, one of the passengers was a cousin of Captain Dick's, who was able to tell him that he was living not far from Falmouth, and it was soon after landing there that Uvillé was able to meet Trevithick, in May 1813, and tell him of his project. Trevithick soon became enthusiastic and made great efforts to get the required machinery designed and built with the utmost despatch. There were delays and there were difficulties with money, but by 1st September 1814 the equipment (four pumping engines with pitwork, four winding engines, a portable rolling mill engine, with much else besides, including four spare boilers) was shipped on board a South Sea whaler and, with Uvillé and three Cornishmen, left Portsmouth for Peru. Some of the engines worked quite well at the Pasco mines but many problems arose, due in part to the local conditions and transport difficulties, but also to the lack of experience and knowledge of the men who had been sent out with the machinery. They would have done a good job under Trevithick's supervision, but not on their own.

TREVITHICK IN PERU

Trevithick made up his mind to go to Peru himself, and moving his family to Penzance, he set sail from there accompanied by a lawyer, Page, and a boilermaker, in the South Sea whaler *Asp* on 20th October 1816.

He was received in Peru with great honour, and he set about making his engines and other equipment work properly, but in this he was before long frustrated by jealousies within the company. Uvillé, who had appeared to welcome him with great pleasure, found that he was himself no longer so highly regarded since Trevithick's arrival, and did all he could to oppose him. Page took a leading part in the opposition. It appears that Trevithick was very badly treated, his competence and even his honesty doubted, and he left in disgust.

He now travelled widely in Peru inspecting the mines and instructing the local miners in English methods of work. In return for this the government of Peru granted him the rights of possession 'for his own benefit and acccount, of such mining spots as were not previously engaged'. He evidently found several of these but did not have the capital to consider working them for himself, with the exception of a copper and silver mine in the province of Caxatambo. Trevithick began to work the mine but in the unsettled state of the country he was obliged to serve for a time in the army of Simon Bolivar, for whom he had invented and made a carbine: it was cast in brass, stock and barrel in one piece, and with a segmented lead bullet it was capable of inflicting very nasty wounds. He was not a good shot, nor did he enjoy shooting, and after a long time Bolivar allowed him to leave the army. He returned to Caxatambo and recommenced working, but ill fortune struck again with the return to the area of the Spanish army and he was forced to leave that part of Peru, robbed of his money and leaving behind him his tools and £5,000 worth of ore that he had ready to be shipped.

Uvillé died in 1818 and not long after his death Trevithick was back at Cerro de Pasco and soon in control of the workings. He had the backing of the most influential of the adventurers of the company and all at last seemed set fair for success. But this was denied to him; the war of liberation which had been swinging about the country reached the mountainous mining district in 1820, a battle was fought at Pasco and the mine was damaged and machinery smashed (some parts of steam engines were concealed from the forces and there is a report of two of them working in Peru in 1872). An extract from a letter, written by a Lieutenant James Liddell of the frigate *Aurora* to Trevithick's son Francis long after the event, is of interest: '. . . he came to dine with us on board HMS *Aurora* then lying in Callao . . . About a year after this terrible disappointment (the battle at Pasco), the *San Martin,* an old Russian fir frigate, purchased by the Chilean government, sank at her anchors in Chorillos Bay, ten miles south of Callao, and your father entered into an engagement with the government in Lima to recover a large number of brass cannon, provided that all the prize tin and copper on board which might be got up should belong to him. This was a very successful speculation, and in a few weeks your father realized about 2500 *l.* I remember visiting the spot with your father whilst the operations were carried on, and being astonished at the rude diving bell by which so much property was recovered from the wreck, and at the indomitable energy displayed by him. It was Mr Hodge, and not I, who then urged in the strongest possible manner that at least 2000 *l* should be immediately remitted to your mother. Instead of this, he embarked the money in some Utopian scheme for pearl fishing at Panama, and lost all!'

In all the years of her husband's absence in South America, Jane Trevithick remained in Cornwall caring for her family. In the early days Richard wrote to tell of his doings but later he does not seem to have written to her or to any of his friends at home. Francis Trevithick, his son and biographer, stated that during all the years of his absence abroad, his wife and family received no financial assistance from him (though he had paid the rent of the house in Penzance, near the one occupied by Humphry Davy's parents, for a year in advance). Her brother, Henry Harvey of the Harvey Foundry at Hayle, looked after her and set her up with her eldest son Richard junior in the inn at Hayle, and she maintained her children and did all that she could to help with her husband's business affairs at home. She had once said of him that 'he was good-tempered, and never gave trouble in home affairs, satisfied with the most simple bed and board, and always busy with practical designs and experiments from early morning until bed-time. He sometimes gossiped with his family on the immense advantages to spring from his high-pressure engines, and the riches and honour that would be heaped on him and his children, but thought little or nothing of his wife's intimation that she hardly had the means of providing the daily necessaries of life.'

CROSSING THE ISTHMUS OF NICARAGUA

For what we know of his adventures in South America we are dependent on his own letters from the early period, letters written by people who knew him, his own recollections after he returned to England and what he told his son Francis, who published a biography some forty years after his father's death.

Leaving Peru after the disaster at Cerro de Pasco, and passing through Ecuador on his way to Bogota in Colombia, Trevithick met James Gerard, who told him of rich mining prospects in Costa Rica. They went there together—Trevithick could not resist the lure. There were indeed rich deposits in the mountains and they spent some years in the country seeing what had already been done and acquiring for themselves some valuable rights for silver and gold mining. At last they decided to return to England to raise capital for their ventures, and rather than undertake the long journey by sea round the Horn, they decided to cross the Isthmus of Nicaragua on foot. They were the first white men to take this route. The party was made up of Trevithick and Gerard, two boys on their way to school in Highgate, and seven natives, three of whom returned home after helping with the first part of the journey. At one stage they made a raft to avoid the labour of cutting their way along the banks of a river, but this became unmanageable, the party was divided on either side of the river and the raft was swept away

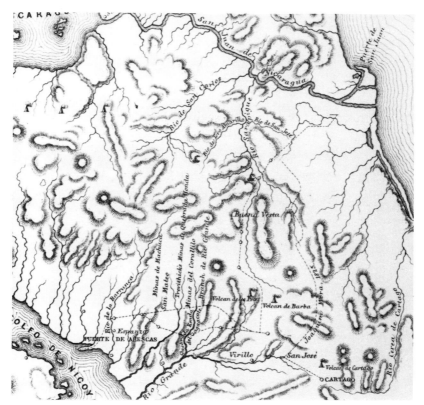

Trevithick's route across the Isthmus of Nicaragua c 1826. It was charted by his son.

by currents. The first thing to do was to unite the party; one man got safely across the river, a second was drowned and Trevithick nearly suffered the same fate but was pulled ashore by the stem of a water plant thrown to him by Gerard when he was all but exhausted. After some three weeks with, as Trevithick said, 'their food monkeys and wild fruit, their clothes at the end of the journey shreds and scraps, the larger portion having been torn off in the undergrowth', they arrived at the port of San Juan de Nicaragua. It is not known how they got from San Juan to Cartagena in Colombia, but a letter written much later describes another narrow escape that

Trevithick had on the way: '. . . if he looked in a sombre and silent mood, it was not surprising, after being, as he said, half drowned and half hanged, and the rest devoured by alligators, which was too near the truth to be pleasant. Mr Trevithick had been upset at the mouth of the river Magdalena by a black man he had in some way offended, and who capsized the boat in revenge. An officer in the Venezuelan and Peruvian services heard his cries for help, and seeing a large alligator approaching him, shot it in the eye, and then, as he had no boat, lassoed Mr Trevithick and drew him ashore much exhausted and all but dead.'

Robert Stephenson, who was on his way home from Colombia, happened to be in Cartagena, and the two engineers met; they had not done so since the time of the Newcastle locomotive, when Robert was little more than a baby and Trevithick sat with him on his knee. He very generously gave Trevithick £50 to help him home, and he eventually arrived at Falmouth in October 1827, his only possessions being the clothes he wore, a gold watch, a drawing compass, a magnetic compass, and a pair of silver spurs.

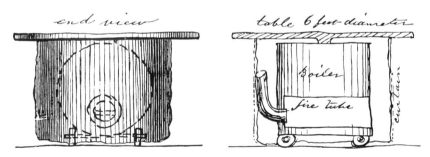

HOT WATER ROOM-WARMER

One of the many inventions that crowded Trevithick's latter years was a portable room heater. A tank of hot water was covered by a wooden table and screened by a circular curtain, making an early form of storage heater.

Return home

MORE SCHEMES AND INVENTIONS

The early part of the nineteenth century had been a time of very rapid development of industry of all kinds, and there had been many changes during the years of Trevithick's absence from England. What had been new, or not even thought of, when he left had become commonplace and, except in Cornwall, his own contributions had been largely forgotten. Even there, though his home-coming was greeted by the ringing of church bells and he was entertained by the gentry, very little was forthcoming by way of reward for the great benefits that had resulted from the use of his inventions.

It was not long before Stephenson's *Rocket,* which henceforth was regarded by most people as the first locomotive, made its debut and the railway age really began.

Richard made considerable efforts after his return, following up those made by his wife Jane during his absence, to obtain payment of royalties that he believed to be due to him for the savings in fuel resulting from the use of his type of engine and boiler. Unfortunately he had little in the way of legal agreements and, apart from one or two small payments, he got nothing.

Later in the year Gerard landed at Liverpool with the two boys on their way to school: he went to see Trevithick and together they tried to interest adventurers in their mining concessions. At one meeting in London Trevithick was offered an immediate payment of £8,000 for his rights but, typically, he turned it down as being insultingly small. Shortly after this Gerard died in Paris and nothing more came of the South American mining adventures.

Trevithick soon turned to new ideas, and they flowed almost as freely as before. In the meantime however, industry generally had progressed a long way, so it was more difficult to make improvements of basic importance. Probably too, he found it much less easy to find either backing for his inventions or firms willing to participate in their development, for few of his ideas of this period were actually made and tested. Some of them were potentially of considerable importance, but little benefit was derived from them by him or anyone else.

The first was a form of gun mounting in which the recoil was to be made to do useful work in putting the gun in position for re-charging; this did not get beyond the making of a model as he could not interest anyone concerned with armaments. Not long after this he was having an iron ship built by Harveys at Hayle—perhaps intended to mount some of his guns, but there is no record that it was ever completed. In the following year he made suggestions for the use of hydraulic power to operate dockside cranes, though this was not a new idea as Bramah had used hydraulic power in 1802.

Another subject which engaged his attention was the expense of bringing large quantities of ice from the Arctic to London, for purposes of cold storage. Writing to Davies Gilbert he made a suggestion for mechanical means of refrigeration; this was then novel and, had he pursued it, he might be remembered as a pioneer in this field too.

Trevithick was invited to Holland in 1828 to investigate the possibility of using the Cornish engine for drainage. That he was still the same kindly and generous (if improvident) man is shown by a story told by his son about this visit: 'He had not money enough for the journey, and borrowed 2 *l* from a neighbour and relative, Mr John Tyack. During his walk home a begging man said to him, "Please your honour, my pig is dead; help a poor man." Trevithick gave him five of the forty shillings he had just borrowed.' His family never knew how he managed to reach Holland, but on his return he told them of the 'honour done him by the King and the kindness of men of influence in friendly communion and feasting'. He made a number of very practical suggestions for draining the submerged land, dredging the Rhine and using the spoil to build dykes round the Zuyder Zee, which could then itself be drained. Though much of this work was not carried out until many years later, Trevithick did design and have built at Hayle both an engine and a ball-and-chain type of pump, suitable for the very low lift required for the work. The balls used in the pump were 3 feet in diameter, probably the largest of its kind ever made. The equipment worked well on trial but in the end never got to Holland because of disagreements between the directors of the company formed to undertake the drainage work.

41

TREVITHICK'S LAST PROJECTS

As he had now abandoned hope of getting any payment from the Cornish mines for the benefit of his inventions, Trevithick set in hand a petition to Parliament for a grant, such as had been made previously to a number of inventors. Whether because Parliament neglected the petition, or did so because it was not presented in the right way is not known, but certainly Trevithick got nothing from it.

He built a successful closed-cycle steam engine in 1829 and followed this with a design for a new type of vertical tubular boiler. A very interesting, though simple, device was invented and produced in 1830: this was a portable room heater. It consisted of a small fire-tube boiler on wheels, with a detachable flue, which could be connected to any convenient fireplace or chimney. There was also an adjustable skirt to control the release of heat from the hot water into the room. The water in the boiler was heated either out of doors or inside with the flue discharging into a chimney, and when it was hot the flue was disconnected, the doors were closed and the heater was wheeled to where it was needed. This had some success and a number were made, some handsomely ornamented with brass. They were early forms of storage heater.

Trevithick's last patent was applied for in 1832; it covered a number of ideas, including among others a water-jet propelled ship operated by an internal reciprocating pump. This was a perfectly sensible idea, but was not built. Also included in the patent were new forms of boiler and superheaters.

Though all his endeavours had been aimed at producing useful works, at the end of his life he designed an enormous column to commemorate the passing of the Reform Bill in 1832. This was to be 1,000 feet high (Nelson's column built in 1849 is only 185 feet) made of 1,500 10-foot square pieces of cast iron, each with several openings in the middle to reduce wind resistance and keep down the weight (which would still have amounted to 6,000 tons). The sections were to be bolted together to make a column 100 feet in diameter at the base, tapering to 12 feet at the top. There was to be an ornamental building round the bottom and a 40-foot equestrian statue on the top, and an air-operated lift was to convey passengers up inside the column. Though there was a good deal of interest in the project and several public meetings were held, it was never built—if it had been, no doubt Trevithick would have been

Trevithick's design for an enormous column to commemorate the passing of the Reform Bill in 1832. Its height of 1000 feet dwarfs St. Paul's Cathedral, the Monument, and the Great Pyramid, which are shown as comparisons.

remembered by many, as the designer of this enormous structure.

At about this time he made an agreement with John Hall, a young engineer who had a works at Dartford in Kent, to carry out some development on an engine there: it is supposed that he was working on a kind of reaction turbine. But he was taken ill, and after only a week of confinement to bed in the Bull Hotel where he had his lodging, Richard Trevithick died on 22nd April 1833. A few days later his workmates carried him to his grave in Dartford churchyard. They are said to have defrayed his funeral expenses.

He was 62 years old when he died. His wife Jane, who had always supported him so loyally, lived on to the age of 96.

43

IN CONCLUSION

Richard Trevithick was one of the very great engineers who lived and worked in England in the eighteenth and nineteenth centuries–comparable in stature with Newcomen, Watt, Smeaton, Telford, the Stephensons and the Brunels. He was a man of very great energy and initiative.

In a lecture to the Institution of Civil Engineers to mark the centenary of Trevithick's death, Professor Charles Inglis ended by saying:

'It is not easy in a few sentences to summarise the versatile and erratic genius of Richard Trevithick. A man of simple tastes, genial, lion-hearted, and without a trace of meanness, in his own county of Cornwall he was looked up to with a veneration which savoured almost of idolatry, but drew the line at votive offerings. Standing head and shoulders above his contemporaries, by indomitable courage, force of personality, and an infinite capacity for hard work, he fought his way to immortal fame practically single-handed. In the brief period between 1799 and 1808 he totally changed the breed of steam engines, from an unwieldy giant of limited ability he evolved a prime mover of universal application.

'Trevithick never sang his own praises, he never boasted about what he had done or what he was going to do; he was essentially a man of actions rather than a man of words. To give material expression to his creative instincts and to see these results in action was to him the salt of life; the acquisition of money was a secondary consideration, only desirable as a means of opening up vistas for self expression in further inventions.'

A few months before his death, in a letter to his old friend Davies Gilbert, Trevithick wrote:

'I have been branded with folly and madness for attempting what the world calls impossibilities, and even from the great engineer, the late Mr James Watt, who said to an eminent scientific character still living, that I deserved hanging for bringing into use the high-pressure engine. This so far has been my reward from the public; but should this be all, I shall be satisfied by the great secret pleasure and laudable pride that I feel in my own breast from having been the instrument of bringing forward and maturing new principles and new arrangements of boundless value to my country. However much I may be straitened in pecuniary circumstances, the great honour of being a useful subject can never be taken from me, which to me far exceeds riches.'

It is of interest to note that several of Trevithick's descendants became well-known engineers, and in particular they worked on the development of the steam engine, boilers and railways in many parts of the world, including Canada, India, Egypt, New Zealand and Japan. His son Francis, who wrote a very full biography of his father was Chief Mechanical Engineer of the London and North Western Railway. His great-grandson, Richard Ewart, was concerned with the design of boilers operating up to 2,000 lb per sq.in. and was present at the 200th anniversary celebrations of his great-grandfather's birth in Cornwall in April 1971.

The monument to Richard Trevithick erected at his birthplace in Illogan, Cornwall.

CHRONOLOGY

1698	*Savery's patent*
1712	*First Newcomen engine at Dudley Castle*
1769	*Watt's separate condenser patent. Cugnot's first steam road carriage in France*

1771	Richard Trevithick born
1777	*Watt's separate condenser engine introduced into Cornwall*
1784	*Murdoch made locomotive model at Redruth*
1790	Trevithick's first employment, as engineer at East Stray Park mine
1792	Trevithick reports on performance of engine at Tincroft mine
1796	First meeting with Davies Giddy (later Gilbert)
1797	Death of his father. Marriage to Jane Harvey. Makes models of high-pressure stationary and locomotive engines
1798	First high-pressure 'puffers' built
1800	*Expiry of Watt patent*
1801	Camborne road locomotive
1802	Granted patent for high-pressure engine, with Vivian
1803	London road locomotive. Boiler explosion at Greenwich
1804	Penydaren locomotive—the first railway locomotive
1805	Newcastle-on-Tyne locomotive built to Trevithick's instructions. Drives a barge by steam engine and paddle wheels
1806	Steam dredger on Thames
1807	Appointed engineer to Thames Archway Company
1808	'Catch-me-who-can' locomotive. Patents (with Dickinson) for steam tug, iron tanks etc.
1809	Patent (with Dickinson) for many improvements to ships etc. Raises a sunken ship off Margate
1810	Typhus and return to Cornwall
1811	Trevithick bankrupt. First Cornish engine and Cornish boiler. Plunger pole engine
1812	High pressure engine applied to agricultural uses. Rock-boring machine for Plymouth breakwater. Screw propeller
1813	Uvillé arrives in England and meets Trevithick
1814	Nine engines shipped to Peru
1816	Sails for Peru from Penzance

1821 Salvage of ship's cargo near Callao
1823 Meets Gerard in Ecuador
1825 *Marc Brunel began Thames tunnel*
1827 Arrives at Cartagena after pioneer crossing of the Isthmus of Nicaragua. Meets Robert Stephenson there. Returns to England. Designs recoil gun carriage
1828 Visit to Holland to advise on drainage. Builds engine and pump at Hayle. Petition to Parliament
1829 Patent for room heater, water-jet propulsion etc.
Stephenson's 'Rocket' won Rainhill locomotive trials
1832 Proposed design for column to commemorate passing of Reform Bill
1833 Richard Trevithick dies at Dartford in Kent
––
1843 *Opening of Brunel's Thames Tunnel*

BIBLIOGRAPHY

Life of Richard Trevithick, with an Account of his Inventions; Francis Trevithick C.E.; E. & F.N. Spon, London, 1872.

Richard Trevithick, the Engineer and the Man; H.W. Dickinson and Arthur Titley; Cambridge University Press, 1934; Trevithick centenary commemoration memorial volume.

The Cornish Giant; L.T.C. Rolt; Lutterworth Press, 1960.

Thomas Newcomen–The Prehistory of the Steam Engine; L.T.C. Rolt; David and Charles, 1963.

The Harveys of Hayle; E. Vale; Barton, 1965.

The Cornish Beam Engine; D.B. Barton; Barton, 1965.

Beyond the Blaze; A Biography of Davies Gilbert; A.C. Todd; Barton, 1967.

The Cornish Miner; A.K. Hamilton Jenkin; 4th edition, David and Charles, 1972.

Industrial Archaeology of Cornwall; A.C. Todd and P.G. Laws; David and Charles, 1972.

INDEX

Page numbers in italic refer to illustrations

Abercynon 21
Bankruptcy 29
Bogota 37
Bolivar, Simon 35, 36
Boulton, Matthew 8, 9, 21, 30, 34
Brunels 26
Callao 36
Camborne *8,* 11, 14, 18, *19*
Carbine 35
Carn Brea 5, *13*
Cartagena 38
Catch me who can 22, *23,* 27
Caxatambo 35, 36
Cerro de Pasco 34-37
Closed-cycle steam engine 42
Coalbrookdale 20
Cold storage 41
Cook's Kitchen *13,* 20
Cornish boiler 29
Cornish engine 30, 41
Costa Rica 37
Cugnot 18
Dartford 43
Davy, Humphry 14, 37
Dickinson, Robert 27, 29
Ding Dong mine 12
Dolcoath mine 12, 17, 30
Drainage scheme 41
East Stray Park mine 14
Falmouth 34, 39
Gerard, James 37, 38, 40
Gilbert, Davies 14, *15,* 17, 18, 20, 21, 24, 33, 41, 44
Goodrich, Simon 26
Greenwich 20
Gun mounting 41
Hall, John 43
Harvey's of Hayle *9,* 14, 37, 41
Hawkins, Sir Christopher 30
Heater, portable *39,* 42
Herland mine 32
High-pressure engines 17, 20, 21, 22, *27,* 31, 34, 44
Hill, Anthony 21
Holland 41
Homfray, Samuel 21

Illogan 5, *45*
Kibbal 15
Lancashire boiler 30
Limehouse 26, 29
Locomotive 17, 18, 21, 22, *25*
Margate 29
Murdoch 17
'Nautical Labourer' 27
Newcastle-on-Tyne 22
Newcomen, Thomas 6, *7,* 8, 9, 11, 12
Nicaragua 37, 38
Penydaren 20, 21, 22
Penzance 35, 37
Peru 34-37
Petition to Parliament 42
Phillips, Henry 32
Plunger pole pump 14, 15, 32
Plymouth breakwater 30, 32
'Puffers' 17
Quarrying 32
Railway locomotive 21, 22, *25*
Recoil engine 33
Reform Column 42, *43*
Rennie, Sir John 30
Road locomotive *16,* 18, *19,* 20
Rotherhithe 26
San Juan de Nicaragua 38
Savery, Thomas 6
Stephenson, George 22, 40
Stephenson, Robert 39
Tanks, iron 28, 29
Thames tunnel 24-26
Threshing machine 30, *31*
Tincroft mine 14
Trevithick, Francis 12, 36, 37, 44
Trevithick, Jane 14, 26, 36-37, 40, 43
Trevithick's parents 11, 14
Tyack, John 41
Typhus 29
Uvillé, Francisco 34, 35, 36
Vazie, Robert 24
Vivian, Andrew 18, 20, 33
Watt, James 8, 9, 11, 12, 14, 17, 18, 21, 30, 34, 44
Wheal Prosper 30
Wrecks, raising 29